Keep this pocket-sized Frith book with you when you are visiting the Cotswolds, or if you are on holiday in the locality.

Whether you are in your car or on foot, you will enjoy an evocative journey back in time. Compare the Cotswolds of old with what you can see today—see how the streets of the towns and villages open spaces have changed; examine the shops and buildings and notice how they have been altered or replaced; look at fine details such as lamp-posts, shop fascias and trade signs; and see the many alterations to the Cotswolds landscapes that have taken place unnoticed during our lives, some of which we may have taken for granted.

At the turn of a page you will gain fascinating insights into the unique history of the Cotswolds.

G000160897

FRANCIS FRITH'S
pocket ALBUM

THE
COTSWOLDS

A POCKET ALBUM

Adapted from an original book by
JOHN BAINBRIDGE

First published in the United Kingdom in 2005 by
Frith Book Company Ltd

ISBN 1-84589-075-2
Text and Design copyright © Frith Book Company Ltd
Photographs copyright © The Francis Frith Collection

The Frith photographs and the Frith logo are reproduced under licence from Heritage
Photographic Resources Ltd, the owners of the Frith archive and trademarks

All rights reserved. No photograph in this publication may be sold to a third party other
than in the original form of this publication, or framed for sale to a third party. No parts
of this publication may be reproduced, stored in a retrieval system, or transmitted, in any
form, or by any means, electronic, mechanical, photocopying, recording or otherwise,
without the prior permission of the publishers and copyright holder.

British Library Cataloguing in Publication Data

The Cotswolds—A Pocket Album
Adapted from an original book by John Bainbridge

Frith Book Company Ltd
Frith's Barn, Teffont,
Salisbury, Wiltshire SP3 5QP
Tel: +44 (0) 1722 716 376
Email: info@francisfrith.co.uk
www.francisfrith.co.uk

Printed and bound in Great Britain by MPG, Bodmin

Front Cover: BURFORD, HIGH STREET C1955 B369011t
The colour-tinting is for illustrative purposes only, and is not intended to be historically accurate.

Frontispiece: CIRENCESTER, MARKET PLACE 1898 40965

AS WITH ANY HISTORICAL DATABASE THE FRITH ARCHIVE IS CONSTANTLY
BEING CORRECTED AND IMPROVED AND THE PUBLISHERS WOULD WELCOME
INFORMATION ON OMISSIONS OR INACCURACIES

MINCHINHAMPTON, VIEW FROM FORWOOD c1955 / M83045

CONTENTS

FRANCIS FRITH
VICTORIAN PIONEER

Francis Frith, founder of the world-famous photographic archive, was a complex and multi-talented man. A devout Quaker and a highly successful Victorian businessman, he was philosophic by nature and pioneering in outlook. By 1855 he had already established a wholesale grocery business in Liverpool, and sold it for the astonishing sum of £200,000, which is the equivalent today of over £15,000,000. Now in his thirties, and captivated by the new science of photography, Frith set out on a series of pioneering journeys up the Nile and to the Near East.

INTRIGUE AND EXPLORATION

He was the first photographer to venture beyond the sixth cataract of the Nile. Africa was still the mysterious 'Dark Continent', and Stanley and Livingstone's historic meeting was a decade into the future. The conditions for picture taking confound belief. He laboured for hours in his wicker dark-room in the sweltering heat of the desert, while the volatile chemicals fizzed dangerously in their trays. Back in London he exhibited his photographs and was 'rapturously cheered' by members of the Royal Society. His reputation as a photographer was made overnight.

VENTURE OF A LIFE-TIME

By the 1870s the railways had threaded their way across the country, and Bank Holidays and half-day Saturdays had been made obligatory by Act of Parliament. All of a sudden the working man and his family were able to enjoy days out, take holidays, and see a little more of the world.

With typical business acumen, Francis Frith foresaw that these new tourists would enjoy having souvenirs to commemorate their days out. For the next thirty years he travelled the country by train and by pony and trap, producing fine photographs of seaside resorts and beauty spots that were keenly bought by millions of Victorians. These prints were painstakingly pasted into family albums and pored over during the dark nights of winter, rekindling precious memories of summer excursions. Frith's studio was soon supplying retail shops all over the country, and by 1890 F Frith & Co had become the greatest specialist photographic publishing company in the world, with over 2,000 sales outlets, and pioneered the picture postcard.

FRANCIS FRITH'S LEGACY

Francis Frith had died in 1898 at his villa in Cannes, his great project still growing. The archive he created continued in business for another seventy years. By 1970 it contained over a third of a million pictures showing 7,000 British towns and villages.

Frith's legacy to us today is of immense significance and value, for the magnificent archive of evocative photographs he created provides a unique record of change in the cities, towns and villages throughout Britain over a century and more. Frith and his fellow studio photographers revisited locations many times down the years to update their views, compiling for us an enthralling and colourful pageant of British life and character.

We are fortunate that Frith was dedicated to recording the minutiae of everyday life. For it is this sheer wealth of visual data, the painstaking chronicle of changes in dress, transport, street layouts, buildings, housing, engineering and landscape that captivates us so much today, offering us a powerful link with the past and with the lives of our ancestors.

Computers have now made it possible for Frith's many thousands of images to be accessed almost instantly. The archive offers every one of us an opportunity to examine the places where we and our families have lived and worked down the years. Its images, depicting our shared past, are now bringing pleasure and enlightenment to millions around the world a century and more after his death.

SLAD, THE VILLAGE 1910 / 62707

THE COTSWOLDS
AN INTRODUCTION

THE COTSWOLDS—*it is an evocative name, which conjures up a delightful vision of the English countryside at its most pastoral: a landscape of rolling hills and meadows, quiet river banks, honey-stoned villages and bustling market towns. The Cotswolds are all of these and more, though the debate as to their exact boundary can be ferocious. It is best to interpret their geographical extent as generously as possible. Similarly, breaking up the area into descriptive regions is also difficult—any divisions proposed in this book are a matter of personal choice rather than anything definitive.*

To travel through the Cotswolds is to wander through several thousand years of our history. This is a landscape largely created by man, with every passing civilisation leaving a mark. The end result we see today is a pleasing confirmation that the human race can sometimes complement nature rather than destroy it. Archaeologists tell us that these high wolds would have been densely settled even in Roman times, though the evidence of antiquity points to the hills and valleys being important to Neolithic man.

The Anglo-Saxons and Normans began the shaping of the towns and villages, with their generous market squares, taverns and fine wool churches. With the passing of the great religious houses of the district the riches of the wool trade were distributed more widely, to the benefit of local communities. It is impossible to underestimate just what a trade this was, both in its original form during the Middle Ages, when wool was England's greatest export, and later when the pioneers of the Industrial Revolution turned their attentions to the manufacture and mass-production of cloth.

Coming to terms with this long history is as much a delight for resident and visitor as the scenery itself—both are intertwined. The Cotswolds are a place to explore, escape into, and linger in. Such is the potency of their magic that visitors return again and again—or settle there permanently.

THE NAME

Originally the name Cotswold applied only to the area around the source of the River Windrush, and then spread south and west over hundreds of years. 'Wold' means hill, therefore to call the Cotswolds the 'Cotswold Hills' is a duplication. The 'Cot' may derive from the same source as 'cote' in Sheepcote—a place where sheep are enclosed, a very appropriate derivation for this neighbourhood. Locals suggest, as an alternative, that the area is named after a Saxon warlord called 'Cod'—Cod's Wold.

THE
SOUTHERN COTSWOLDS

To say that the southern Cotswolds were once the most heavily-industrialised parts of the region would be to give a false impression of the lie of the land. With the mechanisation of the cloth industry, the fast-flowing rivers around Stroud were used to power the mills which manufactured much of the world's broadcloth and other woollen goods. Huge stone buildings were erected to cater for the industrialisation of this traditional Cotswold trade, and cottages crept up the steep hillsides to accommodate the workers who flooded in from far and wide.

But the Cotswolds' contribution to the Industrial Revolution was extremely localised and on a minor scale when compared with the great industrial centres of Lancashire and the Black Country. The surrounding countryside was not overwhelmed by these activities. Stroud itself retains its attractive setting; the valleys and deep dark woodlands thereabouts more than compensate for the slightly urbanised feel of the old mill town. Much of the cloth industry has now disappeared, and the towns and villages that served it have spent much of the last half-century rediscovering and reinventing themselves. New industries such as tourism have developed, for this is a beautiful locality to explore and linger in.

Not all of the settlements in the southern Cotswolds found an importance in only the last two hundred years. Cirencester was the second most important town in Roman Britain after London. It prospered again in the Middle Ages as it exploited the wool industry, spurred on to giddy commercial heights by the monks of the great abbey which dominated the town. When Henry VIII despatched that particular religious house to the history books, merchant adventurers took over. Cirencester's wool church is an architectural reminder of how well they endowed their local community.

Some southern Cotswolds settlements avoided moving so dynamically with the times. There are still the villages and wilder countryside that the march of national history seems to have bypassed. All are extremely photogenic, with links to a quieter past: a reminder that not all of medieval England quite died with the coming of industry. Halt awhile in hamlets such as Duntisbourne Leer, plunge into the extensive woods around Cranham, stroll through the streets of Painswick in the quiet of evening when the tourists have left, or spend an afternoon in Slad, with a copy of Laurie Lee's 'Cider With Rosie' to hand, seeking out the scenes immortalised in that classic autobiography. That is the best way to get a feel for those parts of the southern Cotswolds that the Industrial Revolution missed.

CHALFORD,
ON THE CANAL 1910 / 62712

Amberley straddles high ground to the south of Stroud, amid glorious Cotswold scenery. This old settlement achieved popularity during Victorian times as the setting for the then popular novel 'John Halifax, Gentleman'. Its author, Mrs Craik, lived at Rose Cottage.

AMBERLEY
1901 / 47357

Though the present building is mostly 17th-century, a mill has existed on this site since Domesday. Arlington Mill served the locality as both a corn and cloth mill and has most recently been a countryside museum, with an excellent display about the life and works of William Morris.

BIBURY

ARLINGTON MILL C1955 / B530025

BIBURY
ARLINGTON ROW c1960 / B530002

This fine row of early 17th-century weavers' cottages is now owned by the National Trust. Bibury itself is an amalgamation of several earlier hamlets, which have all merged together to make the glorious architectural composition we see today.

13

Bisley stands high on a hillside to the north of the River Frome;
it has a wonderful assortment of winding streets and rooftops at
different levels, as though the village has grown out of the landscape.
It is a place to linger and explore, with every turn of a street
revealing new delights.

BISLEY
HIGH STREET 1910 / 62697

BISLEY

The fine lines of Bisley Church show that this is another village that earned its wealth from the wool trade, its magnificent spire declaring to the neighbourhood the pride of its benefactors - the wool merchants.

Below the village, seven springs spout a plentiful supply of water. These wells must have been used by locals for generations. The inscription above the springs reads 'Bless Ye The Lord, Praise Him, And Magnify'.

BISLEY
THE WELLS 1910 / 62696

Hidden in woodland near Stroud, Bussage acquired fame in the 20th century as the home and workshop of the renowned glass engraver and stained glass artist Michael Dinkel.

BUSSAGE

THE VILLAGE c1955 / B259026

Not far from Stroud, the village of Chalford clings to the steep wooded hillside of the Golden Valley. Many of Chalford's streets are too narrow and steep to allow cars and are best explored on foot, much as the master-weavers of the cloth trade would have known them. Chalford shows a degree of industrialisation at odds with the rest of the Cotswolds, and its hillsides are crammed with the workplaces and residences of mill workers. Most of the mills are now silent, dedicated to other uses, but the atmosphere of an industrial town persists.

CHALFORD

THE CHURCH 1900 / 45588

The mechanisation of the traditional cloth industry created the Chalford we see today. But other nearby Cotswold villages suffered as traditional methods were abandoned, making them unable to compete with newer technology. This may be why so many neighbouring villages appear to be frozen in time—there was little need and no money to construct new buildings.

CHALFORD

GENERAL VIEW 1900 / 45587

CHALFORD
1910 / 62713

Much of the woollen industry, by which Cirencester prospered, was organised by the monks of the great abbey which was completed during the reign of Henry II. A later king, Henry VIII, dissolved the abbey, and only the Spital Gateway remains. The wool industry was delivered into the hands of merchant adventurers, who built the huge perpendicular wool church that now dominates the town's market square.

CIRENCESTER

CASTLE STREET 1898 40971

CIRENCESTER

*In Roman times Cirencester, Corinium Dubunnorum, was the second most
important town in Britain after London, standing near the Roman roads of
Akeman Street, the Fosse Way, Ermine Street and the older Icknield Way.
Much of south-west England was administered from here. It revived as a Saxon
settlement, but it did not become prominent again until the emergence of the
wool trade.*

Cirencester is another Cotswold town best explored on foot, not least since traffic has increased substantially since this photograph was taken over a century ago. Fine architecture from all periods survives and the town still prospers, thanks to the shoppers who arrive each week on market days.

CIRENCESTER
GLOUCESTER STREET 1898 / 42362

COLESBOURNE

LOWER HILCOT c1960 / C453011

An ancient ford and footbridge, an abandoned cartwheel, and the splash of running water over a tiny weir—this delightful photograph of two stone cottages and their attractive gardens reminds us that the countryside maintained a timeless air even in the hurry of the 20th century.

CRANHAM WOODS

1907 / 59066

A horse-drawn carriage takes a journey into the extensive woodlands of Cranham, Brockworth and Buckholt. A century later this is still one of the most beautiful stretches of countryside in England. In the autumn the beech trees of Cranham turn a glorious gold, attracting visitors from far and wide.

Prinknash (pronounced Prinnage) Abbey is for the most part a very modern building, rising stark from the valley. But the old manor house is a reminder that this is a very old site, dating back to the 16th century. Benedictines returned to Prinknash in the mid-20th century, establishing the world-famous pottery which can be visited.

CRANHAM WOODS
PRINKNASH ABBEY c1965 / C179031

Duntisbourne Abbots was once the property of the Abbots of Gloucester; it is the northernmost of a string of villages lining the River Dunt. Its churchyard, shadowed by the saddle-backed church tower, is one of the prettiest in the Cotswolds, and a good place to linger on a peaceful day.

DUNTISBOURNE ABBOTS

THE VILLAGE c1960 / D161009

Just along the road from Duntisbourne Abbots is the village of Duntisbourne Leer, named after the great Normandy Abbey at Lire which once owned the manor. Not much more than a large hamlet, Duntisbourne Leer is yet another photogenic and thoroughly charming Cotswold village.

DUNTISBOURNE LEER
THE VILLAGE   C1965 / D245013

Fairford was the birthplace of the 19th-century Christian reformer and hymn-writer John Keble, who would often walk along the banks of the River Coln seeking inspiration for his verse. His book 'The Christian Year' led to the birth of the Oxford Movement, and many of his lyrics are still sung in Cotswold churches.

FAIRFORD

RIVER COLN c1955 / F145009

FAIRFORD

THE CHURCH AND THE MILL c1955 / F145001

The joy of Fairford is its ornate wool church, built in the latter part of the 15th century by John Tame, a wealthy cloth merchant. No other church in England boasts such a wonderful array of early stained glass, 28 examples in all, telling the Christian story from the Creation to the Day of Judgement.

From cottage to mansion, the Youth Hostels Association adapted a wide range of buildings for use by their increasing membership. The hostel at Inglesham was modest compared to some, but still provided all the needs of food and bed for the weary Cotswold explorer.

INGLESHAM

LITTLE HOLME YOUTH HOSTEL c1955 / I26001

LECHLADE

Situated near where Oxfordshire, Berkshire and Wiltshire meet is the pretty village of Lechlade, with its fine array of Georgian houses. The church, with its distinctive spire, dates from the 15th century, and dominates the town's market square.

This old Round House was built for the use of the canal lengthmen, who maintained certain sections, or lengths, of the Thames and Severn canal, which started near Inglesham, close to Lechlade.

LECHLADE
THE ROUND HOUSE c1960 / L147026

Minchinhampton's very fine Market Hall dates from 1698, and demonstrates the early prosperity of this important wool town. The nearby post office is surely one of the most delightful of such buildings anywhere in England, situated as it is in a genuine Queen Anne building.

MINCHINHAMPTON

THE MARKET HALL 1901 / 47348

Apart from a plethora of now silent industrial mills, now mostly put to other uses, the steep lanes of Nailsworth are lined with the cottages of former cloth workers. The streets are steep. The steepest, the appropriately named Nailsworth Ladder, is probably 1 in 2.

NAILSWORTH

FROM ROCKNESS 1904 / 53110

The majority of Nailsworth's buildings are less than 250 years old, built for the workers who had a hard life in the local mills. Apart from the local stone, it would be easy to imagine that you had wandered away from the Cotswolds into a Pennine mill town, such is the industrial atmosphere.

NAILSWORTH

WATLEDGE 1904 / 53113

Nailsworth may not be the most attractive town in the Cotswolds, but the student of industrial archaeology will find it a fascinating place to visit. For it was here that the ancient cloth trade of the area enjoyed a mechanised renaissance at the time of the Industrial Revolution.

NAILSWORTH
GENERAL VIEW 1890 / 25172

Northleach is a delightful town, easily missed with the construction of its recent bypass. As with so many Cotswolds settlements, it made its fortune in the wool trade and still shows off the grandeur of those rich and heady days. The Market Square is overlooked by what is arguably the finest wool church in a countryside full of those magnificent buildings.

NORTHLEACH

MARKET SQUARE c1955 / N125013

Painswick—the 'Queen of the Cotswolds'—is situated amid glorious woodland high on the western side of the wolds. Its narrow winding streets have a Dickensian feel, and but for the hum of traffic, it would be easy to imagine yourself back in more gracious times.

PAINSWICK CHURCH

NORTH SIDE 1890 / 25181

Immortalised by Laurie Lee in his autobiography 'Cider With Rosie', Slad and its wooded valley is known throughout the world by millions of readers who have never been there. We may be thankful that the village has managed to avoid the worst excesses of 20th-century development and that it is much as it was during Lee's boyhood. Slad is not the most beautiful village in the Cotswolds. Its setting is not the most spectacular, compared to some of its neighbours. But it does look as though it really belongs to the setting it has. It is a place of pilgrimage for admirers of Laurie Lee's writings—and a delightful day out for anyone.

SLAD

THE VALLEY 1910 / 62708

Britain's most important centre for the manufacture of broadcloth, this mill town sprawls across its wide valley, a huge piece of industrialisation in a wonderfully natural setting. It says a lot for the beauty and resilience of the Cotswolds that the location has not been overwhelmed by the urbanisation of an industrial age.

With the decline of the cloth trade a number of other industries utilised the old buildings, including piano manufacture. The local museum has an excellent section detailing the rise and fall of the Cotswold cloth trade, and much about the important archaeology of the area.

STROUD
BOWBRIDGE 1890 / 25152

RODBOROUGH

THE FORT 1890 / 25162A

By exploring the high ground around the town it is possible to gain some idea of the scale of industrialisation around Stroud. The eye is drawn further afield to the distant Severn Estuary, the Black Mountains of Wales and Exmoor.

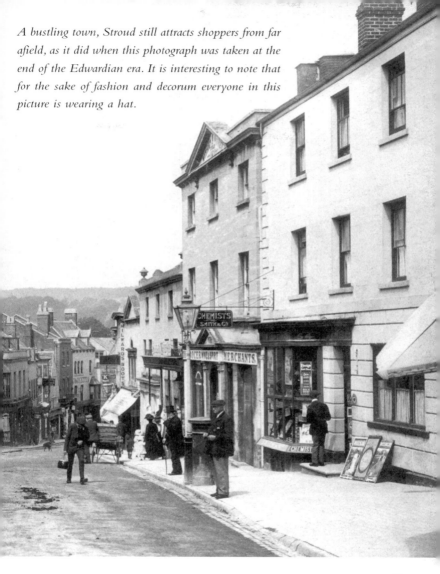

A bustling town, Stroud still attracts shoppers from far afield, as it did when this photograph was taken at the end of the Edwardian era. It is interesting to note that for the sake of fashion and decorum everyone in this picture is wearing a hat.

STROUD

KING STREET 1910 / 62677

Omnibus and bicycle opened up the outside world to many Cotswold villages. For the first time it was possible for shoppers to go into towns like Stroud on a regular basis. This increase in trade helped tide many of Stroud's shops over during the depressions of the 20th century.

STROUD

KING STREET 1925 / 77562

By the 1950s many of Stroud's locally-owned small shops were giving way to familiar chain stores, though the streets remained relatively free of motor traffic.

Tetbury lies near the boundary of Gloucestershire and Wiltshire on the long stretch of high road between Stroud and Malmesbury. It has achieved fame in the last few years by becoming a royal town, for the Prince of Wales lives nearby at Highgrove.

TETBURY

CHURCH STREET c1949 / T155027

Tetbury is one of the statelier towns of the southern Cotswolds, overlooking a tributary of the River Avon. Its location prevented it from being despoiled by the industrialists of the 19th century. Tetbury retains all the charms of a market town from the time of the Stuarts.

TETBURY

GENERAL VIEW C1955 / T155018

As a reminder of Tetbury's wool trade heritage, an annual woolsack race is held up the town's steep Gunstool Hill, each competitor carrying a burden of wool weighing 65 pounds.

TETBURY

BATH BRIDGE C1955 / T155031

*Lying deep in a long valley, Woodchester is
often missed by visitors to the Cotswolds,
but should not be: it has an attractive curved
main street, and some charming old cottages.
The wiser tourist explores the village or sits
to admire the outlook from higher ground,
as this person did in 1890.*

WOODCHESTER
GENERAL VIEW 1890 / 25173

*Woodchester's church, with its dramatic and challenging lines, was
designed and built by the notable architect Teulon in 1863-4.
A prominent monument inside commemorates Wedgwood Allen
of the Royal Flying Corps as a knight in armour.*

WOODCHESTER
THE CHURCH 1890 25174

WOODCHESTER

THE MONASTERY AND ROMAN CATHOLIC CHURCH

1900 / 45592

Woodchester has two monasteries, for Dominican and Franciscan monks respectively. Their Victorian buildings make a dramatic addition to an otherwise quiet and rolling landscape.

CHELTENHAM –
THE WESTERN GATEWAY

There are those who would argue that Cheltenham is not a true Cotswold town, and that this refined and carefully-planned city is geographically an intruder from the Vale of Gloucester. Cheltenham certainly seems at first glance to have little in common with those towns and villages high up on the wolds with their deep valleys, woodlands, meadows, grazing sheep, and buildings that look as though some wild act of geology threw them out of the landscape.

But few would dispute that Cheltenham has long earned its title as the Cotswolds' western gateway. The high viewpoint of Cleeve Hill, popularly regarded as the edge of the wolds, stands proudly above the town, with wide views across the valley of the river Severn to Wales. And many of Cheltenham's buildings are constructed from a similar honey-gold stone familiar to anyone who has explored the loftier landscape to the east of the city.

Cheltenham has, in any case, not always been the fashionable spa we see today. Three hundred years ago, it was a not very distinctive Cotswold village, visited mostly by shepherds with their flocks, stage coaches and sundry travellers on the way to somewhere else. It enjoyed little reputation beyond its fame as a village at the back of beyond. Then the future spa town's first mineral spring was discovered in 1715 by someone with time on their hands, who observed the watering habits of the local pigeons, who always seemed so fat and full of life. A pump room was constructed in 1738, and towards the end of the 18th century King George III gave the growing town the royal seal of approval by taking the waters. Business boomed, and when the town of Cheltenham Spa became a city its grateful citizens incorporated a pigeon into its crest.

Clearly, the old Cheltenham could not provide either the ambience or the facilities to cater for its new upmarket clientele. A calculated campaign of redesign and rebuilding was inaugurated, and this building boom gave us the beautiful and elegant Cheltenham Spa we see today, with its wide avenues, handsome terraces and luxury villas.

The 19th century saw the town expand rapidly as retired empire builders, colonial civil servants and pensioned military officers sought refuge there. Those who were still on active service in far-flung corners of the globe sent their children to Cheltenham, establishing the town's reputation as a centre for education.

Cheltenham is still a busy town with its modern industries, world-famous music and literature festivals, and the National Hunt racecourse—home of the Cheltenham Gold Cup. For the explorer of the western Cotswolds it is a perfect touring centre. Many have begun their love affair with this fascinating and historic region at Cleve Hill, the dramatic backdrop to Cheltenham and its valley. There are few better places to start.

BISHOP'S CLEEVE, THE CHURCH c1955 / B531030

Bishop's Cleeve has now become something of a small town, a dormitory for nearby Cheltenham, but it still has an attractive setting under the slopes of Cleeve Hill. Its fine church was mostly built in the 17th century, though some Norman features remain.

This tall limestone pillar stands above the quarries on Leckhampton Hill, not far from Cheltenham. Much of the stone for the spa town came from this area, and the Devil's Chimney is probably a result of quarrying as well as erosion. There are wonderful views from here across the plain of the River Severn.

CHELTENHAM

THE DEVIL'S CHIMNEY 1901 / 47256

CHELTENHAM
HIGH STREET 1901 / 47265

Not every visitor was impressed by the elegance of Cheltenham Spa. William Cobbett described the town in 'Rural Rides' as 'a nasty ill-looking place', full of "East India plunderers, West Indian floggers, English tax-gorgers… gluttons, drunkards and debauchers of all descriptions, female as well as male'. It was certainly true that fashionable resorts did attract the disreputable in this way.

Cheltenham quickly became a retirement home for officers and colonial administrators, who occupied its Regency terraces and purpose-built villas. In more recent years Cheltenham has established an enviable reputation for fashion and design, for music and literature festivals, and for National Hunt racing on the nearby racecourse.

CHELTENHAM

LONDON ROAD 1906 / 54321

Near to the Promenade is Pittville Park, where Joseph
Pitt established a classically-designed pump room in
the 19th century—the last to be built in the spa town.
Visitors can still take the waters within, while admiring
the fine collection of Regency costumes on display.

CHELTENHAM

THE PROMENADE 1931 / 83808

CHELTENHAM

THE CENTRE 1960 / C75129

By the 1960s, chain stores had become established, even in fashionable
Cheltenham. Happily, many individual shops of fine character selling a
wide variety of goods have survived.

CHELTENHAM

THE COLLEGE 1901 / 47270

Cheltenham has become a byword for public school education in England. Its College for boys, situated on the road to Bath, was built in the 1840s in the popular Gothic revival style. The nearby Cheltenham Ladies' College was founded by the formidable Victorian educationalist Miss Beale.

Even today the College boasts an annual summer cricket festival, in the best public school tradition. At the height of the British Empire, the colleges took in the children of military officers and civil servants posted to far-flung corners of Queen Victoria's realm.

CHELTENHAM

THE COLLEGE PLAYING FIELDS 1907 / 59038

Cleeve Hill is the western edge of the Cotswolds, and at over a thousand feet the highest point. In the far distance are the hills of Wales, the Mendips and Exmoor. Nearer are the Vale of Gloucester, Cheltenham and the flood plains of the River Severn.

CLEEVE HILL

GENERAL VIEW 1907 / 59055

CLEEVE HILL

WASH POOL FARM 1907 / 59060

Prestbury, close to Cheltenham Racecourse, has the reputation of being one of the most haunted villages in England. A cavalier hurries through the streets, a monk haunts shady corners of the village, and a violent phantom hovers to trap the unwary—leaving them all aside, Prestbury is a pleasant place for a stroll.

PRESTBURY

THE CHURCH 1901 / 47300

As the home of such a famous racecourse, Prestbury has been the training ground for many famous racehorses. The tram and cyclists here are heading up the steep ascent of Cleeve Hill, which is not far from the village.

PRESTBURY
THE VILLAGE 1907 / 59051

THE
NORTHERN COTSWOLDS

The northern Cotswolds are a land little changed by time. Take away the ubiquitous motor car from the village streets, and it is quite possible to gaze at the honey-stoned cottages, the winding lanes and ancient churches and imagine yourself back in a very different age.

There is little of the industrialisation of the south, and no large towns such as Cheltenham in the west. The towns of the north and east tend to be small, functional places, owing their original prosperity to the wool trade, but having changed remarkably little since. Burford, Chipping Norton, Stow-on-the-Wold and Winchcombe are old settlements, whose names resonate through English history; some were important in Saxon times, others show signs of the Norman yoke, or battle damage from the Civil War. They survived, and still do today, as market towns - places where it is still possible to hear the Cotswold burr spoken among the myriad accents of visitors from further afield.

The villages are a delight, some of the prettiest in England. Their breathtaking beauty and harmony tempt the traveller to stay for ever. It is easy to understand just why the locals are fiercely loyal to the places where they live. Even in the obvious tourist traps of Bourton-on-the-Water, with its collection of bridges and river scenery, or the Slaughters and the Swells with their picture postcard joys, the attractiveness has remained undiminished, even with their need to cater for so many admirers.

Most villages grew up along the banks of rivers and streams which flow idly, compared to the swifter waters of the south. Old mills survive, powered by water, which serviced the wool and cloth trade as well as the pressing agricultural needs of local communities for centuries. Many streams wind splendidly through the midst of town and village, giving a place to stroll, linger, or just feed the ducks. They have exquisite, evocative names like Windrush and Evenlode - as poetic in name as they are delightful to follow.

Beyond the settlements and river valleys are the high wolds, sheep-grazing land for thousands of years. This is a landscape more ancient than the oldest buildings in the valleys below. It was old when the Romans came, as ancient monuments such as the Rollright Stones suggest. It is a place where humanity has always lived in harmony with the land and nature. Some of the tracks probably date back to that time, making the Roman roads which criss-cross the region look recent by comparison.

This is a pastoral land of wide horizons, where the sky seems to touch the distant hilltops, an enthralling world often deserted except for the grazing sheep and circling birds.

ASCOTT-UNDER-WYCHWOOD

THE VILLAGE c1955 / A140006

Along the Evenlode, that gentle Cotswold stream, stands a string of villages all 'under Wychwood', that ancient wood that still remains one of the most extensive stretches of woodland in Oxfordshire, but which in earlier times was a substantial forest. With its neighbouring village Shipton-Under-Wychwood, Ascott had a reputation for harbouring poachers in earlier centuries.

Bourton-on-the-Water is probably the most popular tourist haunt in the Cotswolds. It deserves its popularity. This stretch of the pretty little River Windrush, the collection of low stone bridges, and a fine village of Cotswold stone, all combine to make a memorable day out.

BOURTON-ON-THE-WATER

THE FOOTBRIDGE 1948 / B392035

Its accessibility from the towns and cities of the Midlands has made Bourton a favourite day out. The village scarcely seems despoiled by having so many admirers. It is still possible to find a quiet corner to feed the ducks, a pleasant shop to browse in, and an ancient inn to enjoy a lunchtime meal.

BOURTON-ON-THE-WATER

THE VILLAGE c1955 / B392038

Rather like Gulliver in Lilliput, the visitor finds an exact likeness of Bourton-on-the-Water in its famous model village. The model village itself has a replica model village and that model village a smaller model village… and so on and so on.

BOURTON-ON-THE-WATER
THE MODEL VILLAGE C1955 / B392051

Traditional English teashops reached their zenith in the peaceful days of the 1950s, having made a comeback after the restrictions and rationing of the Second World War. The neat layout, the ornaments and the rack of postcards—some, perhaps, are Friths—set a standard common to the Cotswolds even up to the present day.

BOURTON-ON-THE-WATER
THE STUDIO CAFE c1955 / B392054

Broadway is a tempting village for tourists, full of antique and craft shops. But its popularity does nothing to detract from the fact that this is an exceptionally beautiful Cotswold village, each building in harmony with its neighbour and all constructed from the same warm local stone.

BROADWAY
THE VILLAGE AND THE NEW CHURCH 1899 / 44115

BROADWAY

A number of the old houses here were originally inns, for Broadway lay on the London to Worcester coaching route. Here we can see the village in quieter days, before the constant stream of cars that flood into Broadway today; the heaviest traffic is a horse-drawn covered wagon.

This tumbledown cottage shows the reality of cottage life in the 19th century, far removed from the romantic restorations that we see today.

BROADWAY

CHINA SQUARE 44117 / 1899

By the 1950s, with the advent of popular motoring, Broadway was starting to attract car-borne tourists in considerable numbers. At about the same time many of the local shops were transformed into cafes and gift shops to cater for this new clientele.

BROADWAY
THE VILLAGE c1955 / B222060

BURFORD

HIGH STREET c1955 / B369011

Sloping gently down to the River Windrush, Burford's High Street is lined with a wonderful variety of old buildings. The discerning visitor with a taste for architecture will wander off into the neighbouring streets—such as Sheep Street—to see Cotswold buildings of the very highest quality.

Burford has not always been the peaceful place we see today. In AD 752 the Saxons defeated the Mercians in a fierce fight in the field close to the church now known as Battle Edge. In the Civil War Oliver Cromwell and Sir Thomas Fairfax incarcerated 340 mutinous troopers in Burford church. Three were later executed by firing squad in the churchyard, and a fourth was made to preach a sermon of repentance, which he did 'howling and weeping like a crocodile'.

BURFORD
HIGH STREET C1960 / B369020

CHIPPING CAMDEN

HIGH STREET c1950 / C335035

*Take away the motor cars and we have a good idea of
how an affluent wool town would have looked during
the 14th and 15th centuries. Grevel House, in
nearby Grevel Street, belonged to the prosperous wool
merchant William Grevel, supposedly the model for
the merchant in Chaucer's 'Canterbury Tales'.*

One of the highest towns in Oxfordshire, Chipping Norton gets the 'Chipping' in its name from the Saxon word for market. Its prosperity dates back to at least the 13th century, though a village stood on this site long before that. Locals rarely call the place anything but 'Chippy'. The Market Square is dominated by this dramatic 19th century Town Hall. Locals and visitors come from far and wide to sample the delights of Chippy's Wednesday market which is held here—much as people have done for centuries.

CHIPPING NORTON
THE TOWN HALL c1955 / C288025

Chipping Norton's church was rebuilt during the days of wool trade prosperity. Legend says that a priest in olden times evicted five devils from the building, pursuing them up to the Market Place and into a flock of sheep. Their five hideous faces gaze down from the vaulted ceiling of the magnificent church porch.

CHIPPING NORTON
CHURCH STREET c1955 / C288032

The present church of St Mary's dates back to the 14th and 15th centuries, with some earlier Norman features. Church Street has eight attractive gabled almshouses, with eight front doors but nine chimneys, dating from 1640.

CHIPPING NORTON
CHURCH STREET c1955 / C288020

CHIPPING NORTON

HIGH STREET c1955 / C288037

The wide central square shows Chipping Norton's origins as a market town. It is still set out with stalls on market days. By the 1950s the town had to cope with increasing traffic, and the square provided a handy solution before the construction of purpose-built car parks.

A wonderful example of Victorian architecture, the Bliss Tweed Mills dominate the approach to Chipping Norton, looking more like a stately home than a factory. The mill was built by George Woodhouse in 1872, on the site of a mill at least a hundred years older. The business continued in operation until 1980; the building has since been converted into luxury apartments.

CHIPPING NORTON
BLISS TWEED MILLS c1960 / C288051

Just south of Chipping Norton is the handsome church tower of the appropriately-named village of Churchill; the tower is a copy of the tower at Magdalen College, Oxford. This quiet village was the birthplace of Warren Hastings, governor-general of India, whose trial and acquittal on charges of corruption was one of the longest legal proceedings in British history.

CHURCHILL

THE VILLAGE AND THE CHURCH c1960 / C290003

In 1769 William Smith was born in a house in Churchill which still survives. Smith produced the first geological map showing England's rock structure, and he is considered to be the father of modern geology.

CHURCHILL

THE CHURCH c1960 / C290001

Nestled in a fold of the Cotswolds, the neat village of Cornwell is one of a piece with the beautiful stone manor house just to the west, providing a unified design rare in Oxfordshire. The manor was restored in the 20th century by Clough Williams-Ellis, the celebrated architect of Portmeirion.

CORNWELL

THE VILLAGE c1965 / C720049

Given the lack of car parking (and who would wish to blight such a perfect spot with parked cars anyway?) the best way to visit Cornwell is to walk or cycle there from Chipping Norton. There are a number of delightful country lanes to explore in the vicinity, where it is possible to get a real feel for the gentle Oxfordshire countryside.

CORNWELL

THE VILLAGE c1965 / C720062

Little remains of the 13th-century Hailes Abbey except the ruins of the cloisters. But there is a wonderfully peaceful atmosphere, and it is easy to see why the monks chose this remote site for their contemplative life. An excellent little museum on the site gives an idea of the majesty of the original buildings and shows off some of the remaining relics.

HAILES

FROM THE EAST 1924 / 76164

Lower Slaughter is best visited on a crisp winter's day, when the stream is full and the houses stand clear against the morning sun. To see this small village in the absence of too many people is to get a feeling of how isolated these Cotswold villages would have been in earlier times.

LOWER SLAUGHTER

THE GREEN c1955 / L313007

LOWER SLAUGHTER
THE MILL AND THE POST OFFICE c1955 / L313010

Lower Slaughter is an artist's and photographer's paradise, with its picturesque stream flowing under attractive little stone bridges. The village's name comes not from some gruesome event in its past, but probably from the Old English word 'sclotre', meaning a muddy place.

Upper Slaughter was the home of F E Witts, the 19th-century parson, who portrayed the village in his 'Diary of a Cotswold Parson'. Witts was a 'Squarson' of the old sort, being both the Lord of the Manor and the rector of this lovely village in its exquisite pastoral setting.

UPPER SLAUGHTER

THE VILLAGE c1960 / U44003

Upper Slaughter's tiny church has been 'restored' on several occasions, not always sympathetically. But it does retain a number of interesting Norman features and a rare 14th century Sanctus Bellcot, which have managed to survive the worst excesses of the Victorian restorers.

Not far distant from the Slaughters are the little villages of Lower and Upper Swell, both situated in an entrancing rural landscape along the banks of the River Dikler. The church at Lower Swell has some fine Norman carving, and is thought to stand on an important Roman site.

LOWER SWELL

THE VILLAGE c1955 / L525011

Visitors' cars are sensibly discouraged from entering the narrow lanes of Upper Swell, leaving this lovely village for the pedestrian to enjoy. St Mary's has an impressive Norman doorway and a 15th-century porch which, happily, the destructive Victorians left alone.

UPPER SWELL

ST MARY'S CHURCH c1955 / U56009

'Stow-on-the-Wold, where the wind blows cold...' runs the ancient rhyme. The highest town in the Cotswolds can certainly be windswept, particularly in the winter. On balmier days it is a good place to halt for a while. Stow is not only an attractive town, but one steeped in the riches of English history.

STOW-ON-THE-WOLD

THE GREEN C1955 / S260003

STOW-ON-THE-WOLD
VIEW FROM THE LYCH GATE c1955 / S260047

STOW-ON-THE-WOLD

THE SQUARE 1957 / S260045

Local lore says that the buildings were clustered so tightly around the Square to keep the wind off the farmers on market days. Daniel Defoe records in his 'Tour of Britain' that 20,000 sheep were sold at Stow-on-the-Wold market in the year prior to his visit.

The English Civil War ended at Stow-on-the-Wold when the parliamentarian Sir William Brereton defeated the aged royalist Sir Jacob Astley in 1646. Some 1600 prisoners were incarcerated in the parish church of St Edward after a last fight at nearby Donnington.

STOW-ON-THE-WOLD

THE SQUARE AND THE STOCKS C1955 / S260010

Stow-on-the-Wold is the junction of eight major roads, including the Roman Fosse Way, and has always attracted travellers from far and wide. This old market cross, with its restored lantern head, must have witnessed centuries of Stow's history.

STOW-ON-THE-WOLD

THE MARKET CROSS c1960 / S260063

Winchcombe lies on the high ground to the north-east of Cheltenham; its street pattern suggests its origins as an important Saxon town, once the capital of the kingdom of Mercia. Its Saxon abbey, the burial place of the Mercian King Kenulf and his son Saint Kenelm, was destroyed during the Reformation.

WINCHCOMBE
THE VILLAGE 1907 / 59456

Winchcombe's long central street becomes in turn Hailes Street, High Street, Abbey Terrace, Gloucester Street and Cheltenham Road, showing off a great variety of magnificent architecture along the way. The Jacobean House in Queen Square is constructed of the same beautifully coloured stone as many of its simpler neighbours.

WINCHCOMBE

THE JACOBEAN HOUSE AND THE CHURCH c1955 / W378002

Winchcombe was the final home of Henry VIII's surviving Queen Catherine Parr, who lived just south of the town at Sudeley Castle. It is unfortunate that her tomb was destroyed during the Civil War, but the town boasts an example of her needlework.

WINCHCOMBE

HIGH STREET c1960 / W378017

*St Peter's Church is all that remains of
the older Winchcombe Abbey, and dates
from the 15th century. Many come
to see the 'Winchcombe Worthies', a
collection of forty grotesque gargoyles
adorning the outside wall.*

WINCHCOMBE

ST PETER'S CHURCH c1960 / W378027

WINCHCOMBE

GLOUCESTER STREET c1955 / W378006

Mingled among the Cotswold stone buildings of Winchcombe are a number of black and white timbered buildings, suggesting the architectural influence of the Vale of Evesham rather than of Cotswold pure and true.

A row of Cotswold stone cottages in Vineyard Street, named after the former abbey's vineyard which was once nearby, built in the style so beloved of all who love the towns and villages of the Cotswolds—and who return again and again.

WINCHCOMBE
VINEYARD STREET c1960 / W378034

It is probable that much of the stone from the abbey
was used to construct and repair buildings in the town.
Seeking out the use of salvaged building materials
makes an unusual and fascinating walk—a good way
to explore the quieter corners of Winchcombe.

WINCHCOMBE

NORTH STREET c1960 / W378019

INDEX

PLEASE HELP US BRING FRITH'S PHOTOGRAPHS TO LIFE

Our authors do their best to recount the history of the places they write about. They give insights into how particular towns and villages developed, they describe the architecture of streets and buildings, and they discuss the lives of famous people who lived there. But however knowledgeable our authors are, the story they tell is necessarily incomplete.

Frith's photographs are so much more than plain historical documents. They are living proofs of the flow of human life down the generations. They show real people at real moments in history; and each of those people is the son or daughter of someone, the brother or sister, aunt or uncle, grandfather or grandmother of someone else. All of them lived, worked and played in the streets depicted in Frith's photographs.

We would be grateful if you would tell us about the many places shown in our photographs—the streets with their buildings, shops, businesses and industries. Describe your own memories of life in those streets: what it was like growing up there, who ran the local shop and what shopping was like years ago; if your workplace is shown tell us about your working day and what the building is used for now. With your help more and more Frith photographs can be brought to life, and vital memories preserved for posterity.

We will gradually add your comments and stories to the archive for the benefit of historians of the future. Wherever possible, we will try to include some of your comments in future editions of our books. Moreover, if you spot errors in dates, titles or other facts, please let us know, because our archive records are not always completely accurate—they rely on 150 years of human endeavour and hand-compiled records.

So please write, fax or email us with your stories and memories. Thank you!

FREE PRINT OF YOUR CHOICE

Choose any Frith photograph in this book.
Simply complete the Voucher opposite and
return it with your remittance for £2.25 (to
cover postage and handling) and we will print
the photograph of your choice in SEPIA (size
11 x 8 inches) and supply it in a cream mount
with a burgundy rule line
(overall size 14 x 11 inches).
**Please note: photographs with a reference number
starting with a "Z" are not Frith photographs and
cannot be supplied under this offer.**
Offer valid for delivery to UK one address only.

Mounted Print
Overall size 14 x 11 inches (355 x 280mm)

PLUS: **Order additional Mounted Prints at
HALF PRICE - £7.49 each** (normally £14.99)
If you would like to order more Frith prints
from this book, possibly as gifts for friends and
family, you can buy them at half price (with no
additional postage and handling costs).

PLUS: **Have your Mounted Prints framed**
For an extra £14.95 per print you can have your
mounted print(s) framed in an elegant polished
wood and gilt moulding, overall size
16 x 13 inches (no additional postage and
handling required).

IMPORTANT!

These special prices are only
available if you use this form to
order. You must use the ORIGINAL
VOUCHER (no copies permitted).

We can only despatch to one
UK address. This offer cannot be
combined with any other offer.

FRITH PRODUCTS AND SERVICES

All Frith photographs are available for you to buy as framed or mounted prints.
From time to time, other illustrated items such as Address Books and Maps are also
available. Already, almost 80,000 Frith archive photographs can be viewed and
purchased on the internet through the Frith website.

For more detailed information on Frith companies and products, visit:

www.francisfrith.co.uk

For further information, or trade enquiries, contact:
The Francis Frith Collection, Frith's Barn, Teffont, Salisbury SP3 5QP
Tel: +44 (0) 1722 716 376 Fax: +44 (0) 1722 716 881 Email: sales@francisfrith.co.uk